ARCHANGELOLOGY
SUN ANGELS POWER

IF YOU CALL THEM THEY WILL COME

KIM CALDWELL

Archangelology LLC

A Division of Archangelology LLC

https://archangelology.com

Introduction Editing and enhancement Rachel Caldwell

Book Editing Grammarly

ISBN: 978-1-947284-42-5

Book Cover Picture Nicola Zalewski

Cover design Kim Caldwell

❀ Created with Vellum

1

ABOUT THE SERIES

"Logic will get you from point A to B. Imagination will take you everywhere."--Einstein

~

This Archangelology book and the entire series aim to lift the reader one step at a time. You may read this piece anytime you desire Upliftment and want to feel good now, never underestimate the power of feeling good for creating more of what you want.

Choose this or any of the other Archangelology Books or Matching Audios to read or listen to for at least 44 nights and raise your vibration consistently for an Uplifted Feeling and Life.

This piece is one of a series of Angelic Upgrade books that fill you with Divine Angelic codes. Angelic laws are based on love and light and thus, operate for free-will, so we must call and ask the Archangels for help.

When working with your book relax, take deep breaths and ground to Mother Earth. Focus on Intentions for whatever it is your heart desires that are for the highest good of all involved. Intentions for these energies that we can not see but feel when we are ready. There are those that believe The Archangels are the Ones that make Law of Attraction Work.

This series of books take on a life of its own as the Archangels move and play from book to book, creating a Delicious Alchemy. Each book becomes an instrument in this Celestial Symphony for a more fulfilling life. Many of the Archangel books also carry and infuse the Violet Flame and Divine Connection to Mother Earth for a transformational experience.

Each book has a matching meditation audio available for your listening pleasure at https://archangelology.com. Please visit our site for your gifts. The book and the audio have similar wording, yet according to the Angels, they Upgrade us differently. Each medium has a unique experience, energetically Upgrading us in distinct ways. Each time you read or hear an Archangel Upgrade, a new dimension is added or adjusted for your benefit.

Become interactive with your book; when inspired, read the words aloud, and let them roll over you, feeling the love and magic that the Angels radiate. When inspired create your own rituals; there is no right or wrong way. As you play with the rock stars of the Celestial realm, you can expect your life to become more heavenly, more peaceful.

You may Notice Many Words are Uniquely Capitalized throughout this series; this is yet another way the Angels infuse us. When you see this try to feel that word or phrase; sensing the depth of its Intensity of Pure Divine Light throughout your Being.

The Archangel Energy is neither male

nor female. This gender fluidity is made clear in this series by the use of the word they or he/she speak to convey a non-gender energy that shifts roles to uplift and nurture you. The upgrades happen in Divine Time, and there is no schedule. There is no competition. There is no rush. Wherever you are in the process is perfect.

A word about the length of this book. "Less is more." This Series of books is the result of decades of study in the art of Law of Attraction, Angelic knowing and energy healing, condensed here for you in a format that will shift and benefit the reader. If you found your way here, you can expect miracles. As Einstein said, "There are only two ways to live your life. One is as though nothing is a miracle. The other is as though everything is a miracle." The matching audio to this book is 44 minutes, so working with that is always an option.

Both Neville Goddard and Albert Einstein stated that our imagination is the creative force. Goddard went so far as to imply that our imagination is the God/dess Energy. I mention this to you because as you read these words with much more than your eyes, let your imagination run wild with vivid pictures of the love the magical Archangels have for you and of your adventures together. Enjoy.

ABOUT THE SUN ANGELS

~

The Sun Angels have come forward at this time to radiate our lives with Sun Power. We may utilize this power to build our health, love, and/or wealth. The Sun Angels do not wish to dictate where this energy flows. They only choose to make the energy available and help us cultivate and channel it. Archangel Metatron comes to play in this book, bringing his connection to Sun Energies and the great King Solomon.

Enjoy as the Sun Angels energize and infuse your chakra system with Sun Codes for Peace, Bliss, Well-Being, and Abundance. Archangels Metatron, Zadkiel, Uriel, Michael, and Raphael join to help the Sun Angels with infusions of the Violet Flame to create powerful Upgrades in all desired areas. Archangel Jophiel and Haniel make guest appearances and help infuse our Solar Plexus with nonjudgement and love, helping us to cultivate confidence and self-love.

All of the Archangels aid in clearing on the Universal feeling of loneliness that humans experience at times. They understand and help clear and heal on the fact that even when other people surround us, we can feel alone. This phenomenon is commonly referred to as feeling lonely in a crowded room. This healing goes through all time, space, and dimensions and helps clear past life feelings that can overwhelm us, unbeknownst to us. This tool of the Archangels will leave us refreshed and renewed. Seraphim Angels also join this healing infusion of Sun energies for the acceptance of self and others, creating more peace and bliss. Archangel Gabriel makes a guest appearance and does a Divine infusing on our throat chakra so we may speak sweet words.

Adapting these mindsets will help shift your consciousness and help you become a magnet for confidence, peace, and prosperity in new refreshed ways. You may read a sentence, a paragraph, or the whole book. It's just whatever you feel you need to embark on this Celestial journey to a more abundant life. There is no right or wrong way to use this tool. All these Divinely Intelligent Angelic Upgrades happen with grace and ease at the individual's comfortable pace. The only thing I recommend you keep in the forefront of your practice is to ensure you are enjoying the process. Meet the Archangels in the Archangelology Book and Audio Series that is here to help you at this time. If you call on the Sun Angels, they will come, just as all of the Archangels will come to your assistance when beckoned. Spending time with Archangels creates a heavenly life.

For gifts from the Archangels visit https:// archangelology.com.

3

SUN ANGELS POWER

~

Archangelology. Sun Angels. Today, we are going to go on a Sunshiny, empowering journey where we will harness the Power of our glorious, life-giving, all-encompassing Sun. Take a deep, healing breath. We will do this with the knowledge that our magnificent Sun is a sentient, intelligent being and that the Sun not only gives life, warmth, and beauty to our lives and our Earth but also can create our personal kingdom. Take a deep, healing breath.

As we go on this journey, we will be accompanied by Divine Beings, the

Archangels. According to ancient wisdom, when we call for the help of the Archangels or any other enlightened beings, they will come to help us. Now, the laws operate with free will; so, we must call, and we must ask these benevolent beings to help us. We will be doing that here today with the intention of bringing the Sun's Power into our lives.

Regarding this Power, we will set our intention, and we can apply it to any area of our lives in which we want a little Sunshine, change, or shift for the better. We will now connect with these Divine Energies. We will rise up out of the fear matrix to a place where we will create with these Divine Sun codes of light. This is where we will create with joy and with ease, where we will connect with the Sun Angels.

Einstein stated that logic would get you from point A to point B. Imagination will take you everywhere. Take a deep, healing breath. Take in this knowing, this knowledge that as we Activate, work with, and cultivate here in this moment, in this Powerful now in our imagination, we are creating, we are bringing in Power, and we are creating our kingdom. Please set your intentions on the kingdom you'd like to create. Maybe you'd like a beautiful home and a family with harmony. Perhaps you'd like an amazing, successful, prosperous business. Maybe you'd like more friends. Perhaps you'd like an exciting love life. Perhaps you'd like more health and vitality. Perhaps you'd like more wisdom and knowing.

Our desires may change from time to time, but know that you can come here or just call in the benevolent rays of light that break up the darkness with our beautiful Sun, and all of your Archangels and your Sun Angels, and you can shift and empower these areas of your life. You are that Powerful, and you are loved and adored by all of these Divine Angels. These Angels have your back. They always have. These Angels want the best for you; so, we will spend some time calling in these Divine Beings so that the rays of Divine Sunlight can shine upon us now. Take a deep, healing breath. I now ask that you call, with me, Archangel Metatron. Archangel Metatron has been associated with Sun energies for centuries. King

Solomon had 44 Seals. One of the Sun Seals of King Solomon was a picture of Archangel Metatron. Whenever we work with Archangel Metatron, just know that Metatron can pull in sacred geometry, Sun codes, and Divine Energies. Take a deep, healing breath.

Now, please see yourself up on a screen, a screen that wraps all the way around. It looks so real; this screen looks beyond real. It brings in crisp colors. You can smell things; you can feel things; all your senses are Activated. Say with me now. "I call on Archangel Metatron to stand before me now." On your other side, please call Archangel Zadkiel. Archangel Zadkiel is the Archangel and Keeper of the Violet Flame. The Violet Flame will transform, transmute, and heal anything that no longer serves you. For example, if you have a memory that hurts to think about, one that seems to keep playing over and over like a loop or like an energy glitch in your mind, we can call on Archangel Zadkiel, and do this with me now. Take a deep, healing breath. Archangel Zadkiel, please be with us throughout this exercise and infuse us and clear us and heal us with your Divine violet flame. Take a deep, healing breath. If there's a memory that keeps popping up, we can call Archangel Zadkiel just as we did and ask Archangel Zadkiel to gently, and with ease, peace, and joy, sizzle that memory away and help it just disappear. Take a deep, healing breath.

Another tool that is ultra Powerful is Ho'oponopono. Ho'oponopono is the ancient Hawaiian Healing art that has been used by masters for centuries. It is the art of making things right, and Ho'oponopono is such a simple, simple process. We simply say, "I love you; I'm sorry. Please forgive me; I forgive you. Thank you." Take a deep, healing breath. We look at that memory, even if it's painful. It could be anything that no longer serves us. It could be worrying about money, it could be worrying about health, or it could be old memories from past lives. As we look upon this, we say, with Archangel Zadkiel and Archangel Metatron standing at our side, so strong, so clear, and so loving, "I love you; I'm sorry. Please forgive me; I forgive you. Thank you." Take a deep, healing breath. As we say this, we see the beautiful Violet Flame melting away anything that no longer serves us, and we know and have great faith that this works. Take a deep, healing breath.

Now, we're going to do some Sun magic. I want you to see the beautiful, magnificent, magnetic Sun glowing high up in the sky. Take a deep, healing breath. I want you to see all the Sun codes and all the sacred geometry going on in the Sun. Yes. Use your imagination. The great Neville Goddard said that our imagination is the God/dess Energy. Become the God/dess Energy now with me. See the Sun glowing, feel the warmth on your skin, and smell the freshness of the air.

Watch as the golden light sparkles around your beautiful Sun. Watch as the rays of the Sun tingle down upon your body. Feel the warmth and notice Archangel Metatron standing right beside you, supporting you, and loving you along with Archangel Zadkiel. This Sun is filled with some amazing qualities. This Sun is filled with love. This Sun is filled with health. This Sun is filled with great wisdom. This Sun is filled with great strength and Power, abundance, kindness, sweet words, bliss, euphoria, and great peace. Take a deep, healing breath.

Now, I want you to direct your attention to your base chakra. This is a glowing energy center at the base of your spine, and I want you to notice it as the Sun starts to move down from the sky. You feel so warm, so light, and so alive, and the Sun keeps moving, moving down. It's getting smaller, and it moves right in front of your base chakra. Repeat after me: "Please stand beside me, Archangel Raphael, as this warm, glowing Sun infuses my base chakra, filling me with abundance, filling me with stability and safety, and filling me with the knowing that I will always have all that I need." Take a deep, healing breath.

Archangel Raphael is the Angel of health and abundance. The Angelic energy is neither male nor female; it is the combination of the God/dess Energy, the Divine Masculine, and the Divine Feminine. Watch as Archangel Raphael points his or her finger right in front of your base chakra and a beautiful, glowing golden ball appears. It's moving, it's full of life, and it is infusing and healing your base chakra now with the Sun energies as Archangel Raphael stands by, supporting you. You're being infused with the knowledge that you'll always have anything you need.

Now, Archangel Zadkiel, the Keeper of the Violet Flame, appears on the other side. You watch as Archangel Zadkiel adds doses of Violet Flame whenever clearing anything that no longer serves you or clearing any fears about security is necessary. Watch as that Violet Flame burns them away in your beautiful base chakra. Watch as Archangel Zadkiel helps to clear any thoughts of scarcity or any thoughts of competition; there is no competition. Archangel Zadkiel reminds you that there is more than enough for everyone. Take a deep, healing breath. At the same time, Archangel Raphael is infusing you with those Sun energies, infusing you with the knowledge that there is more than enough money, more than enough mates, more than enough happiness, and more than enough health. Yes, take a deep, healing breath, and just relax as this beautiful healing is taking place and as these Divine Archangels heal and infuse your beautiful, beautiful base chakra.

Now, notice as Sun Angels start to float down in a circle around you. These Angels are golden, and they're so beautiful; they look like golden light, and their wings look like golden light, and they feel like love. They feel as if the mother, father, and Sun, energy are radiating upon you. You can feel all of this Divine Sunshine, all of these Sun rays, being infused into you now. Take a deep, healing breath and smile; feel how loved and supported you are.

Now, please move your attention to the chakra that is right in between your base chakra and your belly button. This is your sacral chakra. I want you to watch as the Sun above you, that beautiful, whole Sun, starts to drop down again and becomes smaller. Right in front of your sacral chakra is a small ball of shimmering golden light. Archangel Uriel stands right beside you. Say with me now, "Archangel Uriel, please help me bring peace and love into my life." Take a deep, healing breath and watch as Archangel Uriel stands beside you to help you heal and infuse this beautiful chakra.

Your sacral chakra is a beautiful orange color. You can see as this ball, right in front of you, is filled with golden Sun and sacred geometry. You can see it moving, and you see your sacral chakra come to life. Our sacral chakra, when we work with it, can help us heal loneliness. As humans, it is very common for us to go through periods in our lives where, even if we're surrounded by people, we feel lonely. This is natural. It's okay, and now, we're going to use this wisdom and this knowledge, and we're going to ask for the help of the Archangels to help us infuse and to heal this area.

Ask with me now for Archangel Zadkiel to stand beside us and infuse our sacral chakra with beautiful Violet Flames while, at the same time, Archangel Uriel infuses our chakra with loving peace, kindness, warmth, magnetism, and radiance. Take a deep, healing breath. At the same time, Archangel Zadkiel is helping as we pull to mind any times in our life or past lives that we could have felt lonely. Take a deep, healing breath. You're surrounded by Angels now; you're safe.

We are going to put an inner dimensional timeline right at our sacral chakra, with the intention of clearing all of our parallel lives of any times we have felt lonely, we were left by someone, or we left someone. We're going to understand that there are many lives going on at once. These could be called "past lives," "present lives," and "future lives." For the purpose of our work here today, we're going to call these "parallel lives," and we're going to do a simple exercise.

Now, some people can see these other lives that are going on, and some people cannot; however, with the help of the Archangels, the Violet Flame, and the Sunshine Power, we don't have to see these lives. We can just ask for any loneliness that we have going on now or that we have had going on to be healed. We'll also pull in our Ho'oponopono.

If we could see all these lives that are going on all at once, we would understand. Sometimes we're not the good guy; some-times we are the bad guy; sometimes we're the victim, and sometimes we're the good guy; nevertheless, once we understand this, there's no need for judgment anymore. For instance, this is applicable if we have a situation going on where someone leaves us lonely or we feel left out of a group. If we could see these other lives going on, we would understand that there have been times we left others out and want to heal on that as well.

We're going to pull in the beautiful healing of the Archangels, the Violet Flame, and the Ho'oponopono for a simple clearing of loneliness. See your sacral chakra; see that the Sun is glowing, and watch as all the way to the left a line of beautiful golden Sun shoots out to clear and remove anything from any life that is no longer serving you. Then, watch as the line shoots out all the way through the right, through eternity, moving through all lives as all healings are going on now. Take a deep, healing breath. We are clearing and healing future lives with this process as well when we set Powerful Intentions to do so.

Archangel Metatron stands with us now

and helps this inner-dimensional sacred geometric healing that's taking place, and we say to any situations that happen, "I love you. I'm sorry; please forgive me. I forgive you. Thank you." Take a deep, healing breath. Yes; that is wonderful. Archangel Uriel stands strong beside us, his hand at the lower back, supporting us through this healing, infusing our sacral chakra with peace, with knowing that the right people are always coming and that we don't have to settle for anything less than we deserve. Yes; take a deep, healing breath. Sometimes, when we feel alone, we now understand that we're actually surrounded by Archangel Uriel, Archangel Zadkiel, Archangel Michael, and all the Divine, beautiful Archangels. Moreover, all we have to do is ask for their help, and they'll line us up and support us, ever so perfectly, yes.

Now, look up again at the beautiful, beautiful magnetic glitter. Glittering Sun. It's shimmering, it's amazing, it's beautiful. Watch as it slowly drops down again, and you feel the warmth. Yes, feel it on your face. Feel it on your body, warming you. Healing you, yes, and this Sun is moving right down in front of your belly button. Our solar plexus is about confidence, it's about judging ourselves too harshly, and it's about judging others too harshly. We are going to ask the Divine Archangel Jophiel to help us with this magical chakra infusion. Deep healing breath.

Now, look up from your screen at everything that's all around you. The colors are amazing, and you can feel the energy just crackling with life in front of you. It's sizzling, exciting. And see before you, yourself up on the screen, and see Archangel Jophiel right in front you. See her/him clear as a bell. Let your imagination run with this, and repeat after me, "Archangel Jophiel, please stay with me and help me heal loneliness in my life. Help me become magnetized with confidence." Deep healing breath.

Archangel Michael is standing on the other side. Archangel Michael is the amazing Angel of protection who cuts cords for us and who keeps us ever so safe. "Please help me heal, and infuse my solar plexus." Now, watch right in front of you as your solar plexus is glowing, as it's moving, and as it's being infused. You see Archangel Jophiel right in front of you, pointing his or her Divine Finger toward your solar plexus, and you can see it being infused with confidence, tolerance, deep self-love, forgiveness for others, Divine timing, and knowing that everything is in Divine order, and we don't have to judge anyone or anything. Take a deep, healing breath. Look at your belly button area, watch as the Sun's shiny ball just glows and infuses your whole body, and feel your confidence. Feel your Power, and feel the ring of Sun Angels all around you. Now, we're seeing Seraphim Angels start to drop into the picture. There are Seraphim Angels all around you. These Seraphim Angels are infusing you with confidence, health, vitality, knowing, and feeling so great about yourself that you never have to judge another person. Take a deep, healing breath. Any time you get the urge to judge yourself harshly or judge anyone else severely, pull in the knowledge that in all your other lives, you know that, sometimes, you're doing things you're not proud of. We all do, we're human, and it's alright. We can let all judgment go now.

We see these things, and we know in our gut that we don't need to judge anymore. We can pull in our Ho'oponopono, and we can say this to the situation or the person that we unconsciously start to judge. We'll just say, "I love you. I'm sorry, please forgive me. I forgive you. Thank you." Deep healing breath. Yes, and just feel as it melts away. Every time we use this process and call on our Angels to release the judgment, we get better at it. Every time we release judgment, our health improves, and our lives improve. It is such a Divine Process and so worth our time. Deep healing breath.

Now, look up at the sky, at your beautiful Sun, again. Metatron is near the Sun; you can see her/him with her/his beautiful white wings tipped in gold. You notice that the Sun starts coming to you again, and it stops right in front of your heart, right in front of your heart chakra. Deep healing breath. Now, Archangel Haniel is the Archangel of Love, and she/he wants to help us infuse our heart chakra with all the Divine

Love, with all the sacred feelings, with all the sacred knowings that in all our parallel lives, sometimes we have left people, and sometimes they have left us. When we have that feeling of longing, like we need someone and that we can't live without them, and we're so sad because they have left our life, or when we have that feeling of guilt from leaving someone else, this can be overwhelming. We're going to ask that Archangel Haniel and Archangel Zadkiel to help us clear these feelings now.

As the beautiful Sun energies arrive in front of our heart chakra, we watch as Archangel Zadkiel infuses the whole area with Violet Flame, helping us to let it go. Archangel Haniel starts to put beautiful sacred geometry codes into the area of our heart chakra. Archangel Haniel is infusing our heart chakra with love, peace, wisdom, and knowing, and at this moment, we see light—golden Sunlight—shoot out all the way to the left, all throughout eternity and all the way to the right. As all our Sun Angels and Seraphim Angels watch, a beautiful heart chakra clearing is happening in all our lives, throughout all time and space dimensions.

All those times heartbreak occurred, all of those are being cleared out now as we relax and feel the support of the Angels. Archangel Haniel is now also clearing out all competition in our lives on all timelines. There's no need for competition; there's more than enough Infinite Love for everyone.

Archangel Haniel now infuses you with the knowing that perfect loves are always coming to you, so there's no need to cling to anyone or anything that no longer serves you. Take a deep, healing breath. Yes. Now watch again; look up in the sky. As your beautiful Sun starts to move down again, right in front of your throat chakra, Archangel Gabriel wants to infuse your throat chakra with Sweet Words, Angelic Words, with the wisdom to say nice, kind things, and with the wisdom to know when Not to speak. Sometimes the most intelligent thing to say is nothing.

Martial artists are amazing, and they're so strong that some of them could do harm to others with their skills. In their training, the biggest wisdom, the biggest knowing, is not to be involved in a fight, so we ask that Archangel Gabriel infuses us with this wisdom. We know now that we can walk away from a fight, or we can just become quiet and let arguments go. We can ask to be healed of that Universal need to be right or be heard. Archangel Gabriel infuses us now with the knowing that we are loved and supported, and the Angels hear us. They hear when we call. The Sun Angels hear when we call. When we call for Sweet Words, when we call for sweetness, when we call for kindness, all the Angels are listening, and they will bring it to us. All we need to do is clear our throat chakra and gently ask. Yes, ask with me now, "Archangel Gabriel and the Seraphim Angels and my Sun Angels, infuse my throat chakra with Angelic words, words that lift others, words that lift myself, words that heal my world and heal myself." Yes, deep healing breath.

Now, watch as that Sun energy moves right in front of your third eye. Our third eye, as we learn to work with it and Activate it and open it, is so valuable to us. It gives us seeing that helps us to see our Angels. It helps us to see the "unseen." It helps us to see which way to go in life to have a beautiful day, to have an amazing life, and to have a beautiful kingdom, a kingdom that we deserve. Archangel Raziel would like to help us infuse that now. Archangel Raziel is the Archangel of wisdom. Deep healing breath. Archangel Raziel was the Angel known for helping the amazing King Solomon. King Solomon became one of the most prosperous kings in history, and we're going to ask the same Angel that helped King Solomon to help us now. Say with me now: "Archangel Raziel, please infuse my third eye with wisdom, with the Divine Compass and connection to the Divine Intelligence, and with knowing." Yes, see as that beautiful chakra right in front of your third eye glows with beautiful Sun codes, and as your Sun Angels and the Seraphim Angels infuse that chakra, bring it to life, heal it, and feel. Take a deep, healing breath. As your third eye gently opens with ease, with grace, with joy, and with its Divine Timing, there is no hurry. Yes, take a deep, healing breath.

Now, look up again and see your beautiful, warm golden Sun moving down, right above your head, to your crown chakra. Take a deep, healing breath. Right above your head, we're going to work with this Divine Chakra. We're going to go with the wisdom and understanding that this chakra can pull in Divine Healing Energies to help keep us vital, to help keep us youthful, to give us a youthful mind and a youthful body. It is shielding us from any energies that would tell us that we are not perfectly Divine and healed in every moment as we connect to the Divine, beautiful Energies, and we feel these energies infusing our crown chakra now. We see this crown chakra as a thousand-petal lotus, and it's moving in a circle, and it's lighting up with different Divine colors, and we see the golden Sun and all the Sun codes infusing it with the help of Archangel Metatron. We see the Seraphim Angels infusing our crown chakra as it lights up and as we call for any energies that we need. Now, if you need energies to help with anything to be healed, call them in now. If you need energies to help with more vitality, with more energy, with healing the whole body system, call them in now and ask for the support and help of Archangel Metatron with these Divine intelligent Sun energies. Yes; take a deep, healing breath.

Now, your whole beautiful chakra system is running smoothly and infused with Divine Sunlight. Feel this moment. Feel your health; feel your vitality; feel every cell in your body being infused with this Divine, healing Sun Power, Sunlight, and know that the Archangels support you and love you so much in every moment. Know that they are here for you always and supporting you and loving you. Also, each day, look up at your beautiful free supply of gorgeous Sun and Create Your Kingdom.

Thank you, beautiful Archangels. Thank you, beautiful Sun Power. Thank you, Seraphim Angels. Thank you, beautiful Violet Flame. Thank you, Ho'oponopono. Thank you.

4

BONUS CHAPTER ON THE ANCIENT HAWAIIAN ART OF HEALING HO'OPONOPONO

From the Book and Audio Program Activate Your Abundance By Kim Caldwell, available at Archangelologydotcom

Tools for Our Toolbox

ANCIENT HAWAIIAN SECRET

Ho'oponopono

"To be wronged is nothing unless you continue to remember it." ---Confucius

When we experience negative thoughts about someone, we are in that moment holding ourselves away from everything we want. If we happen to desire to be free of this person, we are actually creating an energetic link that is stronger than steel. We are all going to have these thoughts from time to time as we are human, but whether we entertain them or not is up to us. It is in our best interest to clean them up. Do not be hard on yourself for these unwanted thoughts; simply make the decision to stay conscious and lift yourself as often as possible.

Ho'oponopono has been practiced by Hawaiian masters for centuries. Ho'oponopono is the art of sending forgiveness and love to any unwanted situation or person around you. **This begins with the powerful understanding that peace beginswith me.** Understanding that everything in our life is a reflection of what is going on in our heart and mind. Once we realize this, we are in our power. **We do not have to look to one other person to change or do something different in order to thrive. We may take full responsibility for any situation in our lives and clean it up. This is where our true power lies.**

The process is very simple. When we think about an unwanted situation or person, we say to ourselves "I love you," "I am sorry," "Please forgive me," "I forgive you," "Thank you." This immediately starts cleaning and clearing negative memories and emotions from us. This in turn will clear out old conscious and subconscious programs, creating a new space for wonderful new thoughts and blessings to come.

You may be asking, "Why should I take responsibility, when it is the other person's fault?" **This is where we separate the victims from the powerful creators.** Once we start taking full responsibility and realize our true power to clean up everything in our life, we are on our way to true peace of mind and blessings. **When we think negative thoughts about another person or situation, the reason it feels so bad is because this is a departure from whom we truly are and where our power lies. We really feel our best when we are sending love and thinking thoughts that uplift us and others. When we uplift another, we uplift ourselves.** It really is that simple. As we clear years of old accumulated negative thoughts with Ho'oponopono or any other powerful techniques, we are opening up our mind to pure brilliance.We start to be on the receiving end of magnificent ideas. Empowering ideas we never even considered concerning well-being, relationships and income will flow to us. It is not us having these ideas, but the Divine Mind flowing through the clear channel we have created with Love. We can see things in a whole new way when we release resentments blocking our well-being and abundance. The windows become clear and we can see things in a fresh new light. It will become so obvious what a Divine being we are when we pair with God/dess and clear our channel.

This is our birthright. Would you allow some negative thoughts about another to keep you from it? This is big: release these negative self-destructive thoughts and experience more of the abundance and happiness we deserve. It is a constant process, as we are all human and going to have negative judgments. We can, however, lift our minds on a consistent basis, get conscious and reap the never-ending dividends.

Another wonderful technique we can use

is to "turn light" on a person. For example, let's say we are having problems with a good friend, family member or even a "perceived enemy," we can simply say:

Light switch on me (say your name*), and light switch on them* (say their name*).*

So, for example if I am having "perceived" problems with Sally, I would say, "Light switch on Kim, light switch on Sally." Have faith because it is working miracles on subtle levels. Every time you think the negative thoughts, say itagain, "Light switch on me, light switch on them." Always say your name first remembering that you are protected and guided.

Do this for yourself. As we release resentment and negative feelings, we will feel better and set a shining example for those around us. We will no longer be part of a "herd" mentality that says, "It is the other guy's fault." Does it ever do any good to blame others? We are becoming far too smart to continue to blame others and expect things to change. Align your mind-set with the knowledge that when you forgive and love others, you are consciously lifting yourself to the beautiful place you deserve to be. "I love you," "I am sorry," "Please forgive me," "I forgive you" and "Thank you" are words to live by. We are on your way to true peace and blessings.

5

ANGELIC HABITS

There is a saying that our habits make us who we are.

The habit of calling in our Angels creates more peace and poise. As we stop, take a deep breath and call our Angels, this is an opportunity to ground into the now moment and, if we are really on our game, also ground into our beautiful mother earth.

Calling our Angels takes practice and forethought it is a wonderful way to calm fear or anxiety. Acknowledging this Angelic Support allows us to see perceived "challenges" as opportunities. Reminding us that we are never alone and are supported by the

Celestial Masters, the Archangels, and much more.

Make reminders for yourself in convenient places where you will see them stop, breathe and call your Angels.

Do you have an event coming up? Call your Angels now and let them line things up smoothly for you. Allow the Divine Intelligence of the universe to help you.

Please be patient with yourself and with your Angels. Let attachment to outcome go, and as they say, "go with the flow."

Please remember that Angels are on Divine Time, so let go of when you think things "should happen" and allow yourself to relax. Play with this and have fun just like you did as a kid. You can do it and enjoy the process.

6

_____

ANGELIC MANIFESTATION
JOURNAL BONUS

Create more of the life you want with the Archangels as you explore and focus with your Angelic Journal. If you are ready, let's set intentions now to make your Archangel Michael Book a Manifestation tool. It is said that humans have so many thoughts going on in our heads at once that it is hard for Angels and Spirit Guides to hear what we want help with. This is one of the many reasons it is so powerful to get very clear on what we desire and write it out in a designated journal for our Archangels. This way, they can understand our needs better and help us with our dreams and goals in Divine Time.

It has been proven that when we write things down, more of what we desire comes to us. Goals get accomplished, and things flow with more ease. Adding the Amazing Archangels to your journaling just makes the results that much stronger. As we set intentions for what we want and take the time to focus and write it down in our journal, unseen forces move on our behalf. We are going to enlist the help of this Divine Knowing with our Archangel book in an interactive way and turn our book into a manifestation tool. We are also going to play with our books like children and have some fun. Children are powerful creators, and we will take on some of their great habits for their creative value.

Focus and underline ideas you resonate with in your book and become immersed in Upliftment. There is a deeper connection as we become interactive with our Archangel books. We may get colored pens and underline areas of our book that feel important or special to us. We may want to draw pictures of desired blessings or anything that makes us feel good. We may want to mark different areas of our book with hearts, stars, or Angel wings. Get sticky tab notes, a personal favorite, and stick them to your favorite pages you want to return to often. In your journal section, place a sticky tab on an area you want to let the Angels know to help you write in and as a personal reminder. Let your Angelic interaction and intuition guide you with what feels best. Neville Goddard and Albert Einstein both explained that our imagination is a creative force and can bring great blessings to our lives. We will bring our imagination fully into our process now. You may want to add stickers to enhance pages. Place a beautiful angel or magic looking card in your book as a bookmark. Get creative and give your book some personal character. Putting clover or flowers in your book to press and dry, adds some powerful nature magic to your process. Roses are a great choice as they have the highest vibration of any flower. You may give lovely flowers as an offering to your Archangels as well. Giving back is always a beneficial activity.

Everyone has magical abilities. Some of us know this, and some do not. My point is all these ideas are simple and will work for anyone who puts forth an effort and has the faith to relax and let go so the angels may do their work. Of course, anything we put out comes back to us, so we want to always include "for the highest good" in all requests.

In all my studies of magical herbs, cinnamon is found in many different traditions for enhancement of all things wanted and removing things not wanted. You may want to rub a dab of cinnamon mixed with a touch of olive oil on your journal in an intentional shape such as a heart for more love or the infinity symbol for more abundance. Then say to yourself, "I anoint my journal with success and happiness with the help of the Archangels." Anointment has been practiced for eons with much luck and advancement. Basil and Sage could just as easily be utilized. Anything that feels magical and speaks to you in your spice cabinet most likely has wonderful magical properties. Use these gifts of nature with intention and focus for a more joyous life. The idea is to create a magnet for all you desire that is for your highest good with your Archangel Journal.

You may want to underline ideas in colors that mean something to you. The sky is the limit, get creative and juicy with your book, knowing that amazing things are being created.

Next, we have dedicated pages that are waiting for you to fill them with your heart's desires that Michael will help you achieve as long as they are for the highest good. You may write anything you want in your Archangel Journal. There is no right or wrong way to do this. You may ask the Archangels to help you release things from your life, share your hopes and dreams, or ask questions. I love to ask my angels questions and patiently wait to know they will lead me to the answer in Divine Time. Be open and honest with your journaling and the Archangels understanding that the only ones who need to see your Angel Journal are you and your Angels. Keeping your wishes to yourself is very powerful for manifesting as well.

We have created categories for you, and

of course, there will Be freestyle areas, so play with this and have fun. After you play with your journal, you may put it away in a sacred space knowing all is in Divine Order. Remember, magic works just in its own time and asking where the results are will only block things, so relax, have faith, and patience. You may come back to read your Archangel book and add more to it at any time. Know that unseen beneficial forces are moving to help you now and forevermore. Play with and collect other Archangelology books and audios, remembering, "If you call them, they will come." Check out the Archangelology Archangel Journaling Book for more ideas on taking your Journaling Process to the next "celestial" level. The Archangels have tied this whole series Together for us in such a Divinely Intelligent way. Spend time in nature with your book, filling it with love, imagination, and Angelic magic for exponential results. You are a powerful creator and loved by all that is.

Write on the blank areas of your book and on the lined journal areas. Think

outside of the box and let your kid like creative energies flow. Have fun, and add your own flair.

Please enjoy the process and expect wonderful things.

7

SUN POWER JOURNALING

Take a moment to relax and connect with the Sun Angels' Energy. As you get in a still, quiet place, listen for any messages they have for you and journal them here. Let your imagination paint vivid pictures of you and your glorious, dazzling Sun angels playing together in the bright sky. Allow a sweet smile to form as you connect to your Power.

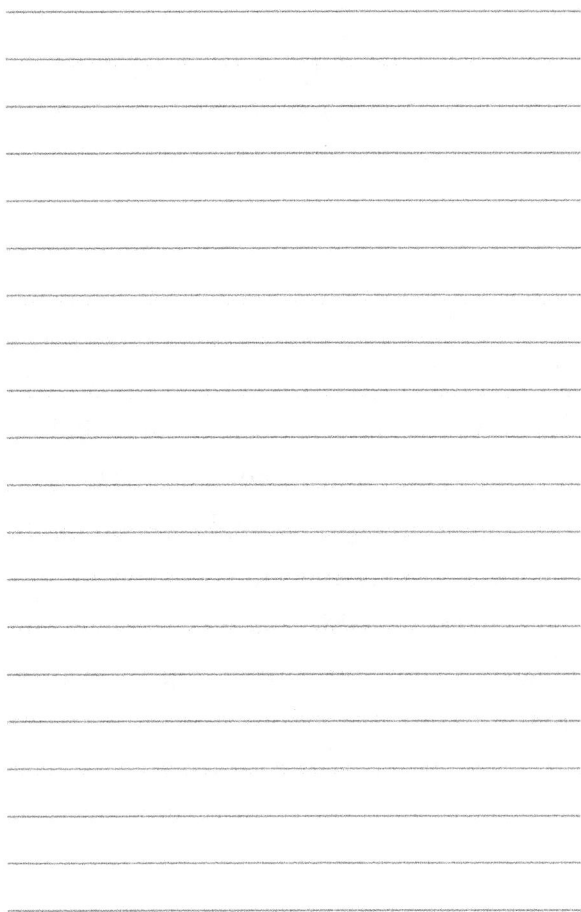

8

CALL THE SUN ANGELS TO EMPOWER YOU

C all in the Sun Angels for anything you would like more Power with. Feel as warmth fills your Mind and Heart, and a secret smile emerges. Journal how you would like the Sun Angels to add Power to your life. Get creative with this. You may want the Sun Angels to help you with a project, relationship, or more self-empowerment. All ways are correct. So enjoy the process.

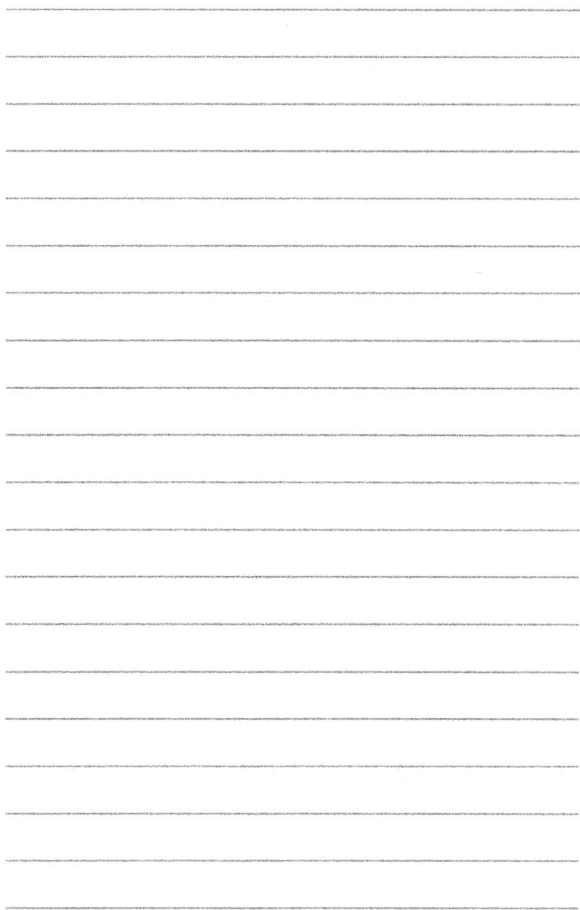

9

CALL THE SUN ANGELS AND ARCHANGEL METATRON TO HELP BUILD YOUR "KINGDOM"

C all in the Sun Angels to help you create your own Kingdom. Ask Archangel Metatron to bring their Sacred Geometry to shimmer divine symbols in your energy field and your world for more blessings. Watch as the Sun Angels and Archangel Metatron stand around you, shimmering you with golden Sun Power to create more benefits in your life—Journal all the Sun Power you would like directed at your Kingdom.

10

SUN ANGEL POWER WITH KING SOLOMON

King Solomon was one of the wisest and most potent of creators. Allow Archangel Metatron to bring their Sacred Geometry and align with Archangel Raziel. Archangel Raziel is the Archangel of wisdom. Relax as Archangel Metatron, Archangel Raziel, and King Solomon to bring Angelic wisdom to your life. Journal how you would like this Divine Wisdom to benefit you and your entire circle of influence. Write how you would like these divine beings to help you.

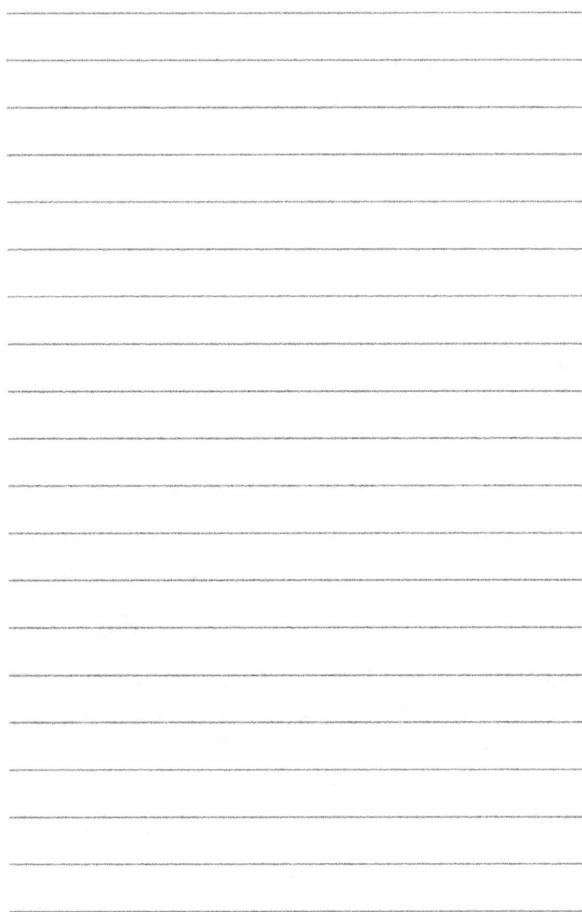

11

BRING THE SUN ANGELS AND
THE VIOLET FLAME TOGETHER

List ways you would like Archangel Zadkiel and their Violet Flame to play with the Sun Angels for Archangel Alchemy. The Violet Fire can clear and upgrade anything in your life by simply saying, "I am the Violet Flame in Action. I am the Violet Flame; I am the Light of God/dess Creation. I am the Violet Flame. I am, I am, I am, I am, I am the Violet Flame. Practice flowing your Violet Flame to any place you plan to go with The Sun Angels. Bring these mighty Angels and Violet Fire into your life and journal about it in creative ways.

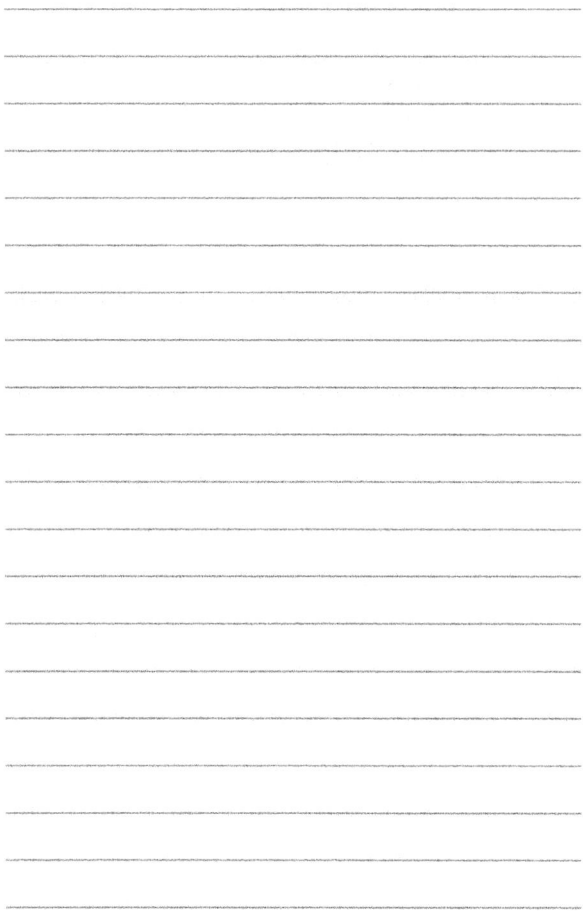

12

FEEL FORTUNATE WITH ARCHANGEL RAPHAEL AND THE SUN ANGELS

Feel the Golden Sun Angels standing around you, feel their warmth, and feel Archangel Metatron standing beside you and supporting you. Call Archangel Raphael to join the party and shimmer you with more Abundance. Allow this Imagination Creation to flow to your journal and express all the Fortune you feel as you bring the Sun Angels and Archangel Raphael into your life to create more. Allow the knowing that the great Archangels surround and support you to fill you.

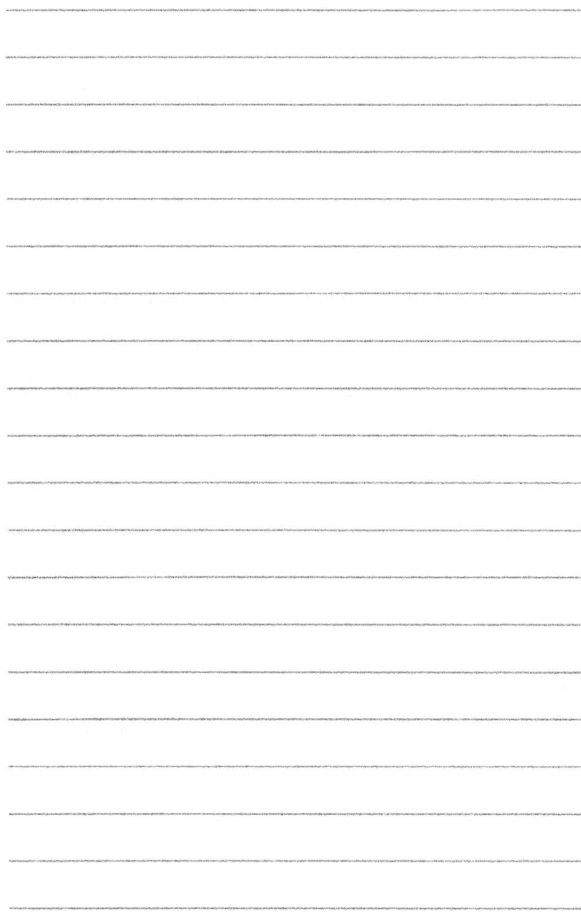

13

CALL IN ARCHANGEL HANIEL WITH THE SUN ANGELS FOR MORE POWERFUL SELF LOVE

Call Archangel Haniel to come in with the Sun Angels to bring more loving Power to your self-love and relationships. Archangel Haniel is the Divine Archangel of Love, and as you combine their sparkling pink energies with the golden sprinkles of energy from the Sun Angels, Archangel Alchemy happens. Journal all the ways this magical Angel energy can help you.

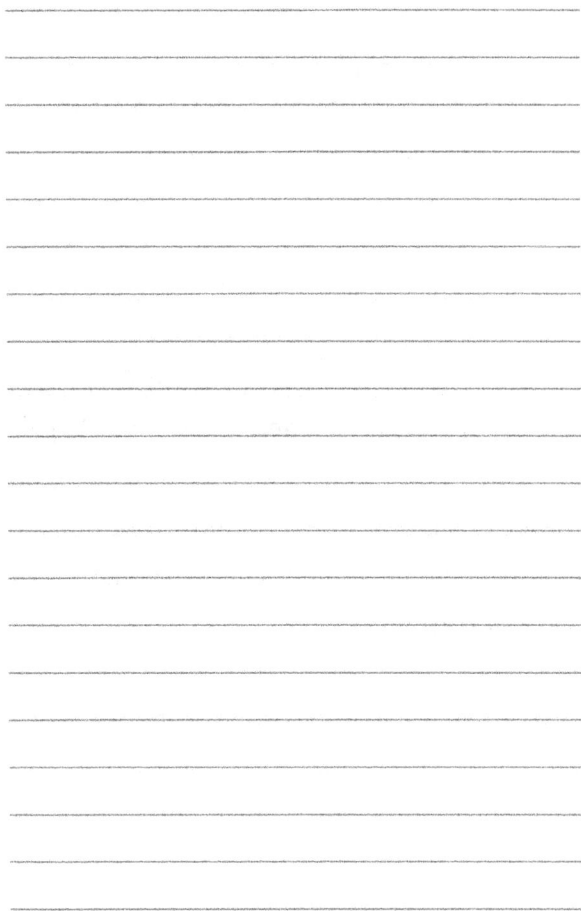

14

BRING ARCHANGEL URIEL AND THE SUN ANGELS TOGETHER FOR POWERFUL PEACE

Allow Archangel Uriel, the Archangel of Peace, to help the Sun Angels empower more Peace in your life. Call on these Angels and direct them in your journal to where you want more Powerful Peace in all areas of your life.

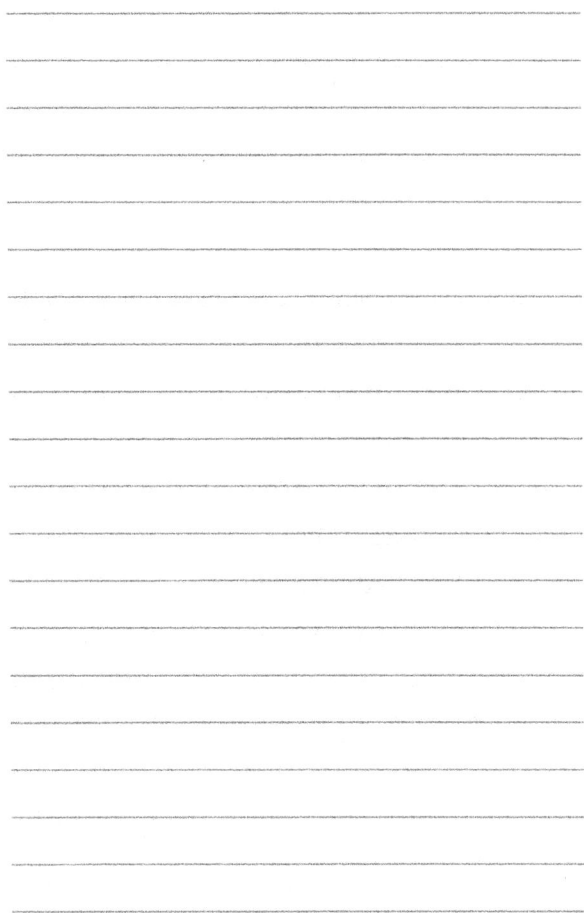

15

BRING HO'OPONOPONO AND
ARCHANGEL ZADKIEL TO PLAY
WITH THE SUN ANGELS

Practice journaling and speaking the Ho'oponopono concerning any situations you want to help. Say, "I love you, I am sorry. Please forgive me. I forgive you. Thank you." until you feel a shift.

Hawaiian masters have practiced this process for centuries to clear and heal any situation. Call in the Divine Archangel Zadkiel, the Archangel of forgiveness, and the Violet Flame for even more power. Feel the Sun Angels bringing Divine Power to the whole situation.

Write all the areas in which you want to practice this beautiful healing phrase.

MORE ANGEL IDEAS

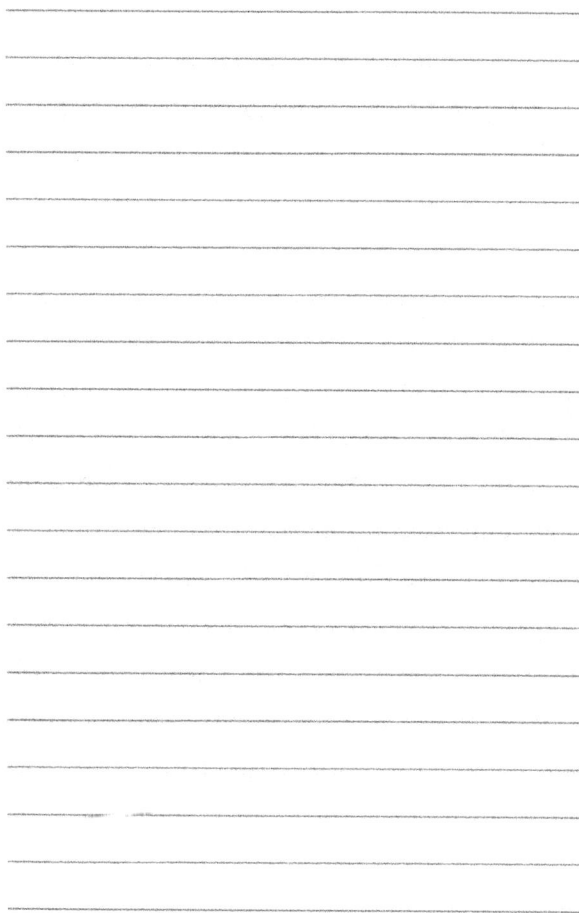

16

ASK ARCHANGEL JOPHIEL TO REMIND YOU HOW SUPPORTED YOU ARE

Call in Archangel Jophiel to come into your life, along with Archangel Michael and the Sun Angels, to stand around you and help you feel all the Angelic Support. Visualize as they infuse you with Angelic sparkles of light and Love. Feel the Seraphin Angels join the party and infuse you with Confidence and Vitality. Journal this imagination creation to feel great.

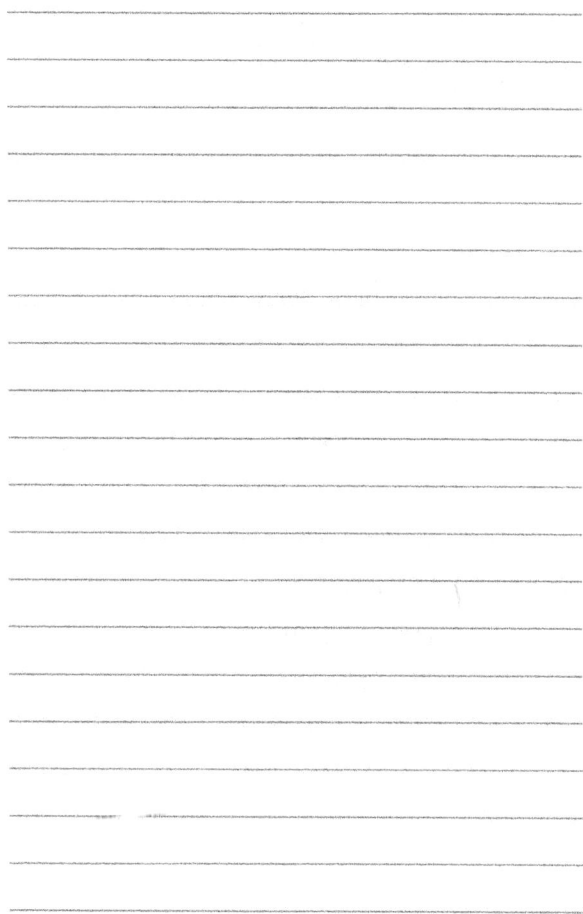

17

GET CREATIVE WITH THE SUN
ANGELS

Fill your Sun Angel journal with bright, creative ideas and pictures. Bring in your childlike enthusiasm to allow more blessings. Call Archangel Metatron, the Archangel of Sacred Geometry, to assist you in finding fabulous new ideas for a more Heavenly Life. Have fun and bring your colored pencils and crayons.

18

ASK THE ANGELS TO REMIND YOU TO CALL ON THEM

W rite different ways you can remember to bring The Sun Angels and all the Archangels into as many moments of your day as possible. Any moment you get still and connect with your Higher Self is an opportunity to see things from your God/dess perspective and bring in blessings. Calling your Angels is a habit that, when cultivated, creates miracles.

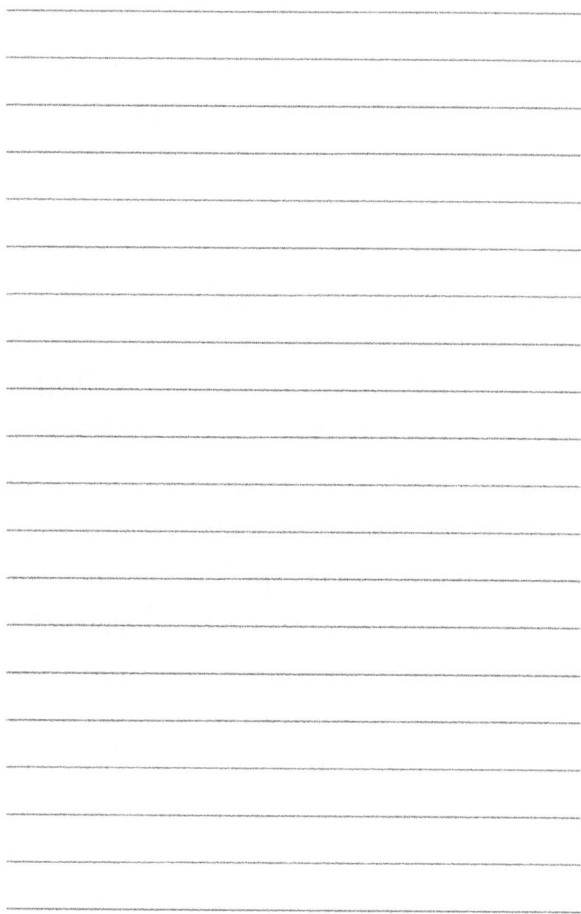

19

ACTIVATE YOUR IMAGINATION
WITH THE SUN ANGELS

Call on the Sun Angels and Archangel Raziel, the Archangel of Wisdom, to help you activate your imagination. See as these Divine beings sparkle you with golden and sapphire angelic sparkles, lifting your energy and making you feel more powerful. Write down all the imagination creations that come to you.

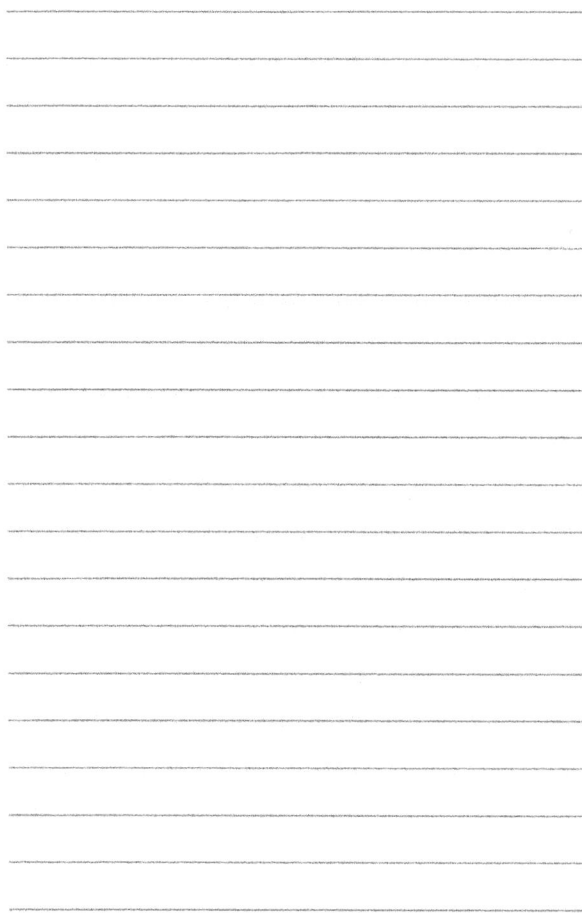

20

CALL IN THE BLUE FLAME
ANGELS

C all in the Blue Flame Angels anytime you would like more freedom, peace, blessings, and Heaven on Earth. Write calls and decrees for the Blue Flame Angels and The Sun Angels here. Get specific with what you would like help with.

Learn more about the Blue Flame Angels here Ascended Masters. Ascended Masters Speak on Angels (Saint Germain Foundation Printing.)

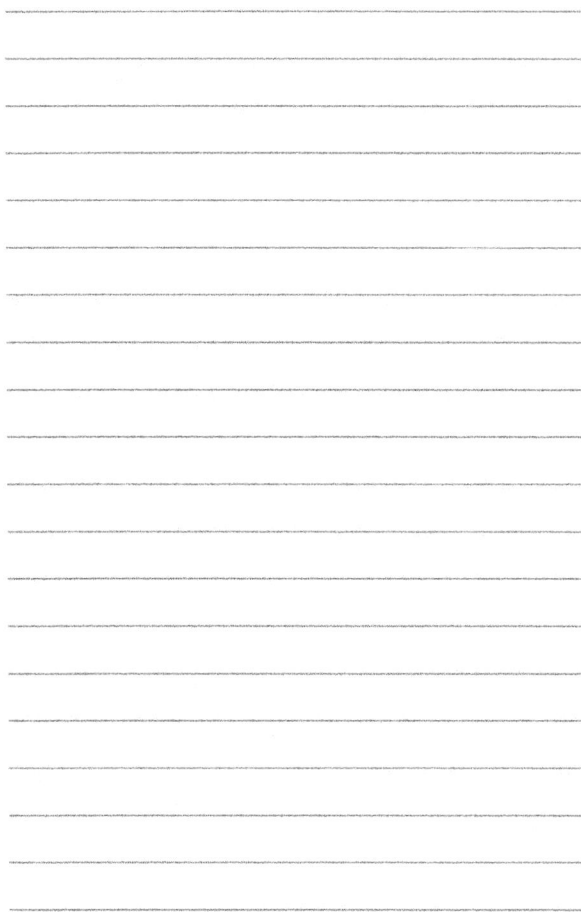

21

BLEND ARCHANGEL ZADKIEL AND THE VIOLET FLAME ANGELS WITH THE SUN ANGELS FOR EXQUISITE POWER

C all Archangel Zadkiel and the Violet Flame Angels to play with you and The Sun Angels. You will be creating Archangel Alchemy at its best. You may visualize the Violet Flame as a carpet spreading throughout your world to bring more Peace and blessings. You may see the Violet Flame coming from your third eye as you spread it through your world. Get creative with these Divine energies and have fun—Journal all your Violet Flame Blessings.

22

LET THE SUN ANGELS FILL YOU WITH MORE POWER

Feel all the Power with the help of The Sun Angels and Archangel Metatron. Allow their Divine Energy to flow to and through you to your Journal.

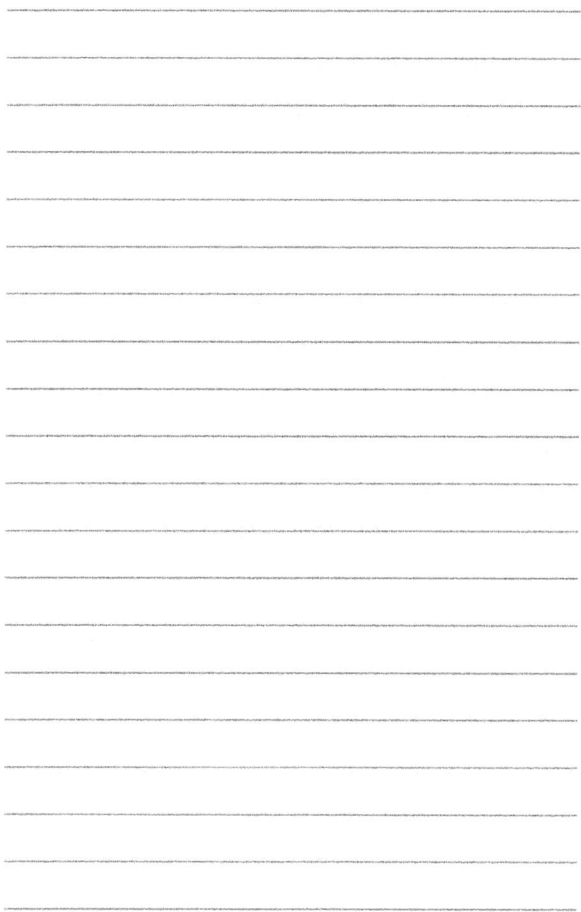

23

CALL ARCHANGEL SANDALPHON FOR MORE HARMONY

Spend time with Archangel Sandalphon and the Sun Angels doing Imagination Creations. Take deep breaths, relax your whole body, and allow the beautiful mind pictures with your Archangel to begin. You can call other Archangels to play with you. Call Archangel Uriel for more Angelic Peace. Call Archangel Camael for more Angelic Courage. There are so many Archangels in this series to call and play with. Have fun journaling about all of them with you.

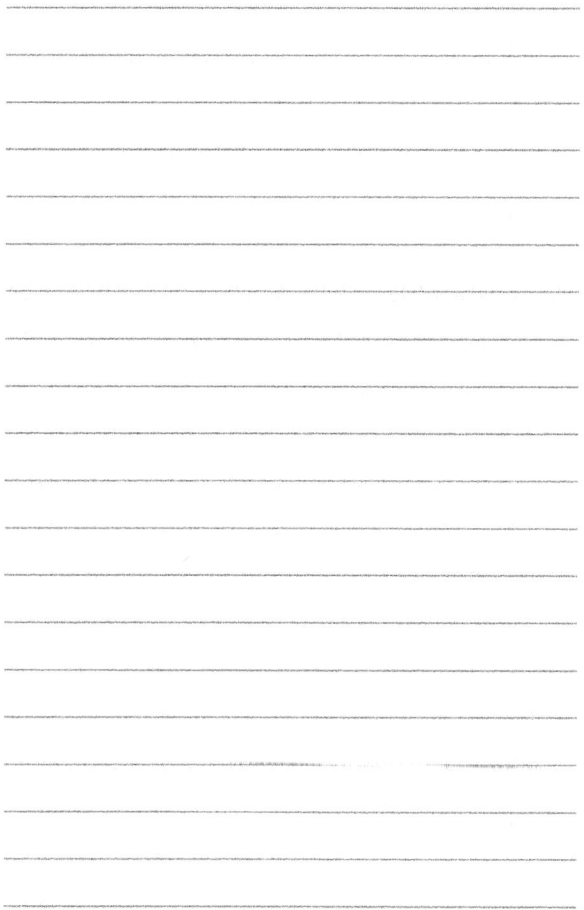

24

BRING IN ST. RITA WITH THE SUN ANGELS

St. Rita is a miraculous Saint who helps grant wishes, among other things. Visualize as St. Rita stands with you and The Sun Angels and shimmers Divine frequencies. Call Archangel Uriel to bring Peace and allow Peace throughout your Mind while you feel calm and blessed. Call Archangel Gabriel to help you feel hopeful in this moment. Journal all the imagination creations you experience with these masters. And remember that Neville Goddard says, "It is the feeling place that creates," so play with feeling your blessings.

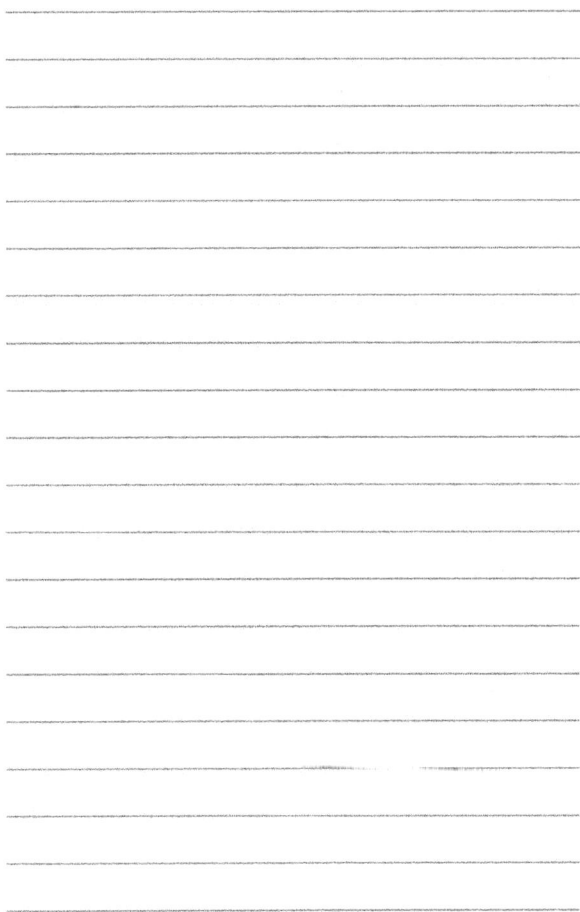

25

FEEL COURAGE WITH ARCHANGEL CAMAEL AND THE SUN ANGELS

Call Archangel Camael to give you more Powerful Courage with the Sun Angels. Feel as Archangel Camael shimmers you with tangerine sparkles of light, encouraging you to love who you are and be yourself more each day. Please remember that you bring great light and blessings to the world just by existing and being you; please remind yourself of this daily. Journal more ways to let your light shine and feel powerful.

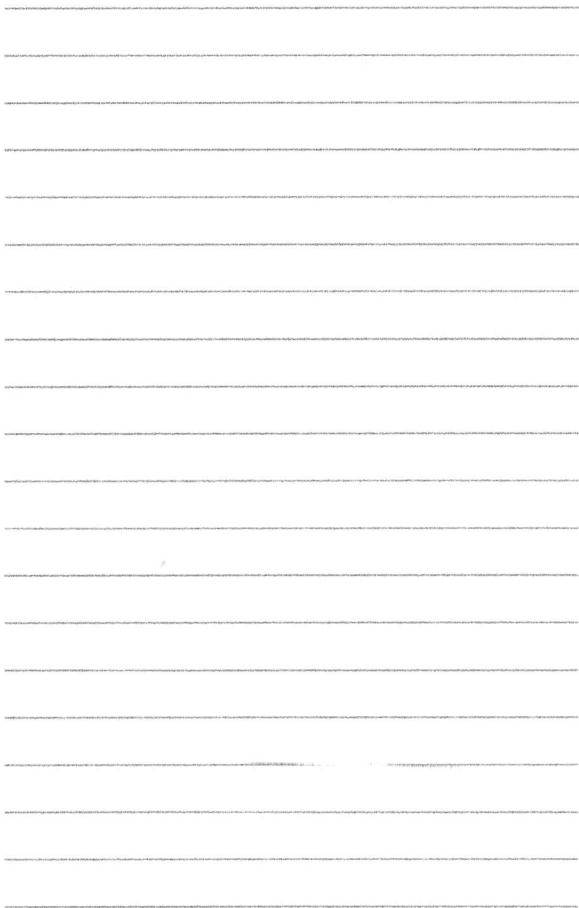

BLESSINGS

May the Divine Creative Force that Moves and Creates the Universes Bless and Enhance Every Wish You Ever Conceived that is for the Highest Good of All Involved. May Joy, Peace, and Purpose Be Yours all the Days of your Lives. Through All Time Space and Dimensions. So, Mote, it Be, and So It Is. I hope this book helps you in wonderful ways and radiates out to a gorgeous life for you and yours. May you always Be Blessed and Highly Favored.

Kim Caldwell, creator of the Archangelology Book and Audio Series

REFERENCES

~

Ascended Masters. Ascended Masters Speak on Angels (Saint Germain Foundation Printing.)

Diana Cooper. The Archangel Guide to Ascension: 55 Steps to Light. (Hay House Inc.)

Matias Flury. Downloads From The Nine: Awaken As You Read. (Matias Flury 2014).

MORE OFFERINGS

~

Visit https://archangelology.com to discover more Archangels and Super Power Saints

Each of the following books has a matching audio filled with healing music.

Archangelology Michael * Protection

Archangelology Raphael * Abundance

Archangelology Camael * Courage

Archangelology Gabriel * Hope

Archangelology Metatron * Well Being

Archangelology Uriel * Peace

Archangelology Haniel * Love

Archangelology Raziel * Wisdom

Archangelology Zadkiel * Forgiveness

Archangelology Jophiel * Glow

Archangelology Violet Flame * Oneness

Archangelology Sun Angels * Power

Archangelology Moon Angels * Magnetism

Archangelology Sandalphon * Harmony

Archangelology Orion * Expansion

≈

The items below come in book only

Archangelology * Archangel Journaling

Archangelology * Archangel Breath-Tap Book

How Green Smoothies Saved My Life Book

≈

Activate Your Abundance Book and Audio Program

≈

The rest of the items below are available in Audio Format

Archangelology*Mary Magdalene*Feminine Divine Audio

Archangelology * Breath-Tap Super Power Saints Volume 1 Audio

Archangelology * Breath-Tap Super Power Saints Volume 2 Audio

Regeneration Meditations * Switchword Series with Solfeggio Frequencies audio

Radiating Divine Love * Switchword Series with Solfeggio Frequencies audio

Love Charm * Switchword Series with Solfeggio Frequencies audio

Dragon Sun Grounding Meditations * Cosmic Consciousness Series audios

Sweet Moon Sleep Meditation * Cosmic Consciousness Series

Enchanted Earth Sacred Geometry * Cosmic Consciousness Series audios

PLEASE WRITE A HELPFUL REVIEW

If you enjoyed this book please give a positive review so others may find it as well. And may blessings come back for your help.

Thank you so much. May you always be Blessed and highly favored.

Kim

9 781947 284425